# THE STORY OF THE

# PITTSBURGH STEELERS

## By Diane Bailey

## BIGFOOT BOOKS

### *The Quest for Discovery Never Ends*

*This edition first published in 2021 by Kaleidoscope Publishing, Inc.*

*No part of this publication may be reproduced in whole or in part without written permission of the publisher.*

*For information regarding permission, write to Kaleidoscope Publishing, Inc.*
*6012 Blue Circle Drive*
*Minnetonka, MN 55343*

*Library of Congress Control Number*
*2020936012*

*ISBN*
*978-1-64519-244-2 (library bound)*
*978-1-64519-312-8 (ebook)*

*Printed in the United States of America.*

FIND ME
IF YOU CAN!

Bigfoot lurks within one of the images in this book. It's up to you to find him!

# TABLE OF
# CONTENTS

# KICKOFF!

It is a little windy inside the Pittsburgh Steelers' stadium. It is not because of the weather. The wind comes from thousands of Steelers fans waving towels! These are bright yellow "Terrible Towels." Fans hope the Steelers will give their opponents a "terrible" time. Often, they do! The Steelers are known for being tough. They are one of the NFL's most successful teams. Let's meet the Steelers!

The Terrible Towels come out when the Steelers take the field!

# Chapter 1

# Steelers History

In 1933, a Pittsburgh businessman named Art Rooney started a football team. He named it the Pittsburgh Pirates. The city was home to many steel factories. In 1940, the team changed its name to "Steelers."

The early years were not very good. The Steelers' first **winning season** was not until 1942. One bright spot was quarterback Bobby Layne. He led the team to some big wins in the 1950s and 1960s. Then things started to go downhill. The team went through seven quarterbacks in five years. They needed a change!

*Bobby Layne practices with John Henry Johnson.*

*A statue of Art Rooney is outside Heinz Field in Pittsburgh.*

# A FAMILY BUSINESS

The Steelers have been with the Rooney family from the start. Art Rooney was the first owner. He passed the team on to his son, Dan. Dan later handed it over to his son, Art Rooney II. Players remember that the Rooneys treated them like part of the family, too. It really is a "family" business!

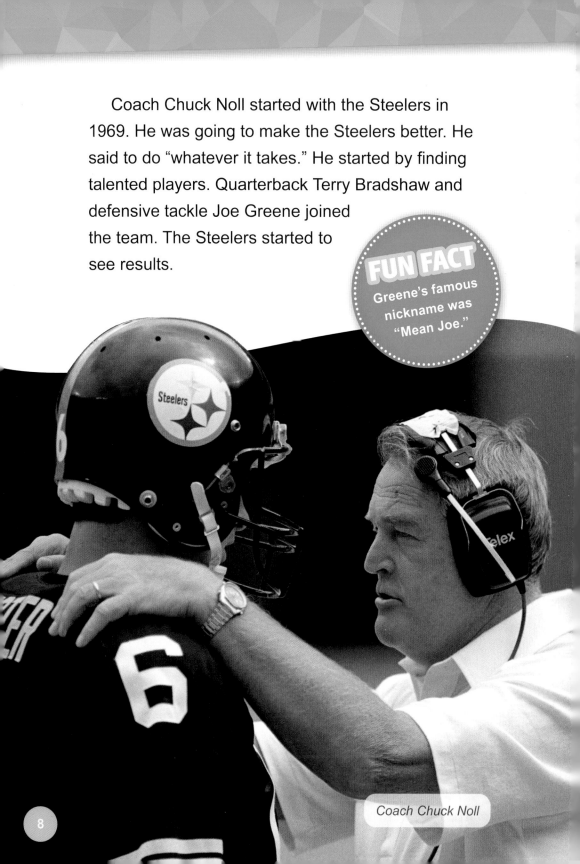

Coach Chuck Noll started with the Steelers in 1969. He was going to make the Steelers better. He said to do "whatever it takes." He started by finding talented players. Quarterback Terry Bradshaw and defensive tackle Joe Greene joined the team. The Steelers started to see results.

FUN FACT
Greene's famous nickname was "Mean Joe."

Coach Chuck Noll

This statue shows Harris making his famous catch.

In 1972, Pittsburgh was playing the Oakland Raiders in the playoffs. The Steelers were losing with only a few seconds left. Bradshaw had to do something, fast! He threw a long pass. A defender knocked the ball off course. The ball did not hit the ground, though. Running back Franco Harris caught it! He ran for a touchdown. Pittsburgh won! It is one of the most famous plays in NFL history.

Pittsburgh's defense led the way in a Super Bowl win over the Cardinals.

## FUN FACT

Pittsburgh's defense allowed only 33 rushing yards to Arizona in the Super Bowl.

The Steelers got even better. Between 1975 and 1980 they won four Super Bowls! They struggled in the 1980s, though. Head coach Bill Cowher was hired in 1992. He took the team to the playoffs six years in a row. They lost every time!

By 2005, the Steelers had turned things around. They made their way to the playoffs. Then they just kept winning! They went all the way to the Super Bowl. They beat the Seattle Seahawks. Coach Mike Tomlin took over in 2007. He led the team to another Super Bowl win in 2009.

The Steelers were back at the Super Bowl in the 2010 season. They hoped to be the first team ever to earn seven Super Bowl titles. Unfortunately, the Green Bay Packers held them off. Pittsburgh lost, 31–25.

The Steelers finished the 2019 season with an 8-8 record. It was not good enough to make the playoffs. The Steelers were disappointed. They knew they could come back, though. They have a winning tradition to continue!

*Mewelde Moore looks for room in the Super Bowl.*

# TIMELINE OF THE PITTSBURGH STEELERS

**1933**

1933:
The Pittsburgh NFL team begins play.

**1947**

1947:
Pittsburgh's first playoff appearance ends in a loss to the Philadelphia Eagles.

**1972**

1972:
After almost 40 years, the Steelers win their division for the first time.

**1974**

1974:
The Steelers get their first Super Bowl win, against the Minnesota Vikings.

**1979**

1979:
A win against the Los Angeles Rams makes four Super Bowl titles in six years.

**2008**

2008:
The Steelers beat the Arizona Cardinals in Super Bowl XLIII. That made them the first team with six Super Bowl wins.

**2010**

2010:
Pittsburgh loses the Super Bowl to Green Bay.

**2017**

2017:
Won 13 games and AFC North title.

# WHAT A CATCH!

Pittsburgh headed to Super Bowl XLIII. They faced the Arizona Cardinals. The game started well for the Steelers. They were ahead 10–7. On the last play of the first half, James Harrison intercepted a pass. He took off for the end zone!

One hundred yards later, he scored a big touchdown!

The Cardinals battled back. Their star receiver Larry Fitzgerald caught two touchdown passes. One of them went for 64 yards. Suddenly, the Steelers trailed!

QB Ben Roethlisberger started to get hot. He completed pass after pass. Time was running out. With just a minute left, Santonio Holmes caught a pass for 40 yards. The Steelers were getting closer to scoring.

Roethlisberger threw the next pass to the end zone. Holmes dropped it!

## FUN FACT

The win over the Cardinals gave the Steelers six Super Bowl wins. No NFL team had ever done that!

Holmes with a toe-tapping, fingertip TD grab!

Pittsburgh had one more chance. Big Ben tossed a ball high in the air. Holmes leaped and caught it! He touched his toes in the end zone before falling to the ground.

The Cardinals could not come back. Pittsburgh won the game!

# Chapter 2

# Steelers All-Time Greats

Quarterback Terry Bradshaw was the number-one **draft** pick in 1970. Coach Chuck Noll knew he wanted him! Bradshaw had a strong throwing arm. He took the Steelers to the top of the league.

Bradshaw had a great partner in receiver Lynn Swann. At the 1976 Super Bowl, Bradshaw threw a 64-yard touchdown pass to Swann in the fourth quarter. It sealed the win over the Dallas Cowboys.

Another great Steelers' receiver was John Stallworth. At the 1979 Super Bowl, Bradshaw threw a short, 10-yard pass to Stallworth. Stallworth ran it the rest of the way. It was a 75-yard touchdown! At the next year's Super Bowl, Stallworth caught a long, 73-yard pass from Bradshaw. He turned that one into a touchdown, too. Another Steelers win!

Terry Bradshaw

Mel Blount

In the 1970s, no team had a better defense than the Steelers. It was called the "Steel Curtain." Opponents could not break through it! It started with Joe Greene. He had a rough style. He could handle two opponents at once! The next year, the "curtain" added cornerback Mel Blount. He was hard-hitting, too. Receivers had trouble getting around him.

Jack Ham and Jack Lambert were tough linebackers. Ham had great **instincts**. He could tell what was going to happen before it did. Lambert signed in 1974. He was Pittsburgh's youngest starter on defense.

The "Steel Curtain" had an amazing year in 1976. Over one nine-game stretch, the defense allowed only 28 points!

Jack Lambert

In the 1990s, cornerback Rod Woodson led the Steelers' secondary. Once he intercepted a pass and returned it 45 yards for a touchdown. That was only the third game of his NFL career! He retired with 71 career picks. Wide receiver Hines Ward is Pittsburgh's all-time leader in receptions. His biggest moment came in the 2006 Super Bowl. Midway through the fourth quarter, he caught a high, 43-yard pass. It clinched the Steelers win.

Running back Jerome Bettis and guard Alan Faneca made a great team. They always knew what each other was thinking. Together, they gave Pittsburgh a fantastic ground game.

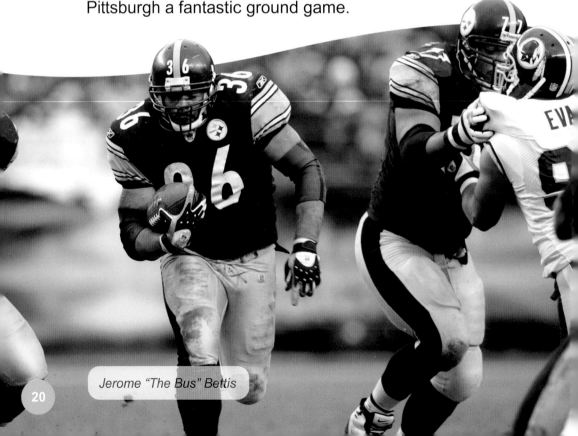

*Jerome "The Bus" Bettis*

# STEELERS

## RECORDS

These players piled up the best stats in Steelers history. The numbers are career records through the 2019 season.

Total TDs: Franco Harris, 100

TD Passes: Ben Roethlisberger, 363

Passing Yards: Ben Roethlisberger, 56,545

Rushing Yards: Franco Harris, 11,950

Receptions: Hines Ward, 1,000

Points: Gary Anderson, 1,343

Sacks: James Harrison, 80.5

# Chapter 3

# Steelers Superstars

Today, the Steelers have one of the league's best quarterbacks. Ben Roethlisberger is bigger than a lot of linebackers! That is why he is called "Big Ben."

Big Ben can use his height to see over the defensive line.

His size makes him tough to **sack**. He can fight off tacklers to find an open receiver. He can run for yards, too. Tackling Big Ben is a big challenge!

Roethlisberger has led the Steelers to three Super Bowls. He has thrown for more passing yards than any other Steelers QB.

**FUN FACT**

Roethlisberger's 5,129 passing yards in 2018 are a Steelers season record.

Running back James Conner is already a winner. In college, he had to battle cancer. He won! He came back to help his team at the University of Pittsburgh win. He joined the hometown Steelers in 2017. When another runner was hurt the next year, Conner was ready to take over. He ran for 12 touchdowns. He was named to the Pro Bowl. That's the NFL's all-star game. No tackler Conner faces is as tough as cancer!

James Conner

*JuJu Smith-Schuster*

In the air, the Steelers depend on their wide receivers. JuJu Smith-Schuster signed with Pittsburgh in 2017. He was the youngest player in the NFL. He became the first 20-year-old player to score three touchdowns.

T.J. Watt causes a Buffalo fumble.

It is hard to get through Pittsburgh's D-line. Defensive ends Cameron Heyward and Stephon Tuitt make a great team. They pressure the quarterback up the middle. Linebacker T.J. Watt plays on the outside. He makes plays that confuse the other team's offense.

Behind the line, cornerback Joe Haden brings a lot of talent and experience. He works well with safety Minkah Fitzpatrick. Both are great at making interceptions. Haden once intercepted two passes in a game against the Arizona Cardinals!

The current Steelers are part of a long tradition. They are talented and tough. They have been through it all—and they are ready for more!

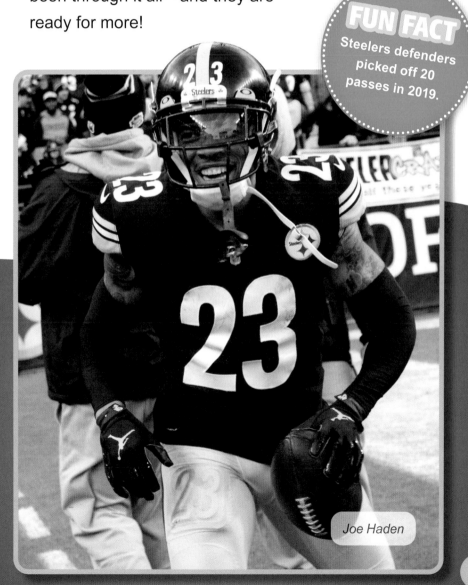

FUN FACT
Steelers defenders picked off 20 passes in 2019.

Joe Haden

# THE BOOK

**After reading the book, it's time to think about what you learned. Try the following exercises to jumpstart your ideas.**

## RESEARCH

**FIND OUT MORE.** Where would you go to find out more about your favorite NFL teams and players? Check out NFL.com, of course. Each team also has its own website. What other sports information sites can you find? See if you can find other cool facts about your favorite team.

## CREATE

**GET ARTISTIC.** Each NFL team has a logo. The Steelers logo shows three colors and cool shapes. Get some art materials and try designing your own Steelers logo. Or create a new team and make a logo for it. What colors would you choose? How would you draw the mascot?

## DISCOVER

**GO DEEP!** As this book shows, the Steelers have a long tradition of winning. A lot of that comes from the Rooney family. They have owned the team since it started. Do some research and look at other longtime NFL owners. Have any others owned their team as long?

## GROW

**GET OUT AND PLAY!** You don't need to be in the NFL to enjoy football. You just need a football and some friends. Play touch or tag football. Or you can hang cloth flags from your belt; grab the belt and make the "tackle." See who has the best arm to be quarterback. Who is the best receiver? Who can run the fastest? Time to play football!

# RESEARCH NINJA

Visit *www.ninjaresearcher.com/2442* to learn how
to take your research skills and book report writing to the next level!

## RESEARCH ...........................

**DIGITAL
LITERACY
TOOLS**

### SEARCH LIKE A PRO
Learn about how to use search
engines to find useful websites.

### FACT OR FAKE?
Discover how you can tell
a trusted website from an
untrustworthy resource.

### TEXT DETECTIVE
Explore how to zero in
on the information you
need most.

### SHOW YOUR WORK
Research responsibly—
learn how to cite sources.

## WRITE ...........................

### GET TO THE POINT
Learn how to express your
main ideas.

### PLAN OF ATTACK
Learn prewriting exercises
and create an outline.

**DOWNLOADABLE
REPORT
FORMS**

# Further Resources

## BOOKS

Hewson, Anthony K. *JuJu Smith-Schuster. Biggest Names in Sports*. Mendota Heights, Minn.: Focus Readers, 2020.

Omoth, Tyler Dean. *The Super Bowl (Sports Championships)*. Minneapolis: Lerner Books, 2019.

Whiting, Jim. *The Story of the Pittsburgh Steelers (NFL Today)*. Minneapolis: Creative Education, 2019.

## WEBSITES

FACTSURFER

Factsurfer.com gives you a safe, fun way to find more information.

1. Go to www.factsurfer.com.

2. Enter "Pittsburgh Steelers" into the search box and click 🔍

3. Select your book cover to see a list of related websites.

# Glossary

**draft:** the annual event at which NFL teams choose college players. In 2020, Pittsburgh did not have a first-round draft pick.

**instincts:** in sports, abilities to predict what is going to happen next. Ham's instincts led him to the right place for the tackle.

**intercepted:** caught a pass intended for the offense.

**sack:** tackle a quarterback behind the line of scrimmage. Pittsburgh lost 10 yards when Roethlisberger was sacked.

**winning season:** a year in which a sports team wins more games than it loses. With a 13-3 record, the Steelers had a winning record in 2017.

# Index

## PHOTO CREDITS

# About the Author

Diane Bailey has written dozens of books for kids and teens, on everything from sports to science to civil rights. She has two grown sons and lives with her husband in Kansas, where they like to watch football, talk about football, argue about football, and look forward to more football!